Scene From
The Movie
GIANT

Tino Villanueva

---

curbstone press

FIRST EDITION, 1993
© 1993 by Tino Villanueva
ALL RIGHTS RESERVED

Printed in the U.S. by BookCrafters on acid-free paper

Curbstone Press is a 501(c)(3) nonprofit literary arts
organization whose operations are supported in part by
private donations and by grants from the ADCO Foundation,
the J. Walton Bissell Foundation, the Connecticut
Commission on the Arts, the LEF Foundation, the Lila
Wallace-Reader's Digest Literary Publishers Marketing
Development Program, administered by the Council of
Literary Magazines and Presses, the Andrew W. Mellon
Foundation, the National Endowment for the Arts, and the
Plumsock Fund.

Library of Congress Cataloging-in-Publication Data

Villanueva, Tino.
    Scene from the movie Giant / by Tino Villanueva. —1st
    ed.
            p. cm.
    ISBN 1-880684-12-8 : $9.95
    1. Mexican Americans—Poetry.   I. Title.
    PS3572.I36S28   1993
    811'.54—dc20
                                                            93-26423
distributed in the U.S. by
InBook
Box 120261
East Haven, CT 06512

CURBSTONE PRESS
321 Jackson Street
Willimantic, CT 06226

acknowledgements:

I wish to thank the editors of the following magazines and anthologies for publishing some of the poems in this book:

The Bloomsbury Review (September / October 1988): "Scene From the Movie *Giant*."
Agni, No. 28 (1989): "Fight Scene Beginning," "Fight Scene, Part II" and "Fight Scene: Final Frames."
Quarry West, No. 26 (1989): "Text for a *Vaquero*: Flashback."
An Ear to the Ground: An Anthology of Contemporary American Poetry (Athens: The University of Georgia Press, 1989): "The 8:00 O'Clock Movie."
Tinta: Revista de Letras Hispánicas y Luso-Brasileñas, Vol. 2, Núm. 1 (otoño 1989): "The Trailing Consequence: A Triptych" and a first version of "Fade-Out-Fade-In."
After Aztlán: Latino Poets of the Nineties (Boston: David R. Godine, Publishers, 1992): "On the Subject of Staying Whole."

*For B. Knott, for the helpful criticism
and encouragement*

*For J. Salinas, who assimilated the
film from the beginning*

These poems tell of an incident past and
are meant to be read in sequence.

CONTENTS

V

Scene From
The Movie
GIANT

Scene from
the Movie
GIANT

What I have from 1956 is one instant at the Holiday
Theater, where a small dimension of a film, as in
A dream, became the feature of the whole. It
Comes toward the end...the café scene, which
Reels off a slow spread of light, a stark desire

To see itself once more, though there is, at times,
No joy in old time movies. It begins with the
Jingling of bells and the plainer truth of it:
That the front door to a roadside café opens and
Shuts as the Benedicts (Rock Hudson and Elizabeth

Taylor), their daughter Luz, and daughter-in-law
Juana and grandson Jordy, pass through it not
Unobserved. Nothing sweeps up into an actual act
Of kindness into the eyes of Sarge, who owns this
Joint and has it out for dark-eyed Juana, weary

Of too much longing that comes with rejection.
Juana, from barely inside the door, and Sarge,
Stout and unpleased from behind his counter, clash
Eye-to-eye, as time stands like heat. Silence is
Everywhere, acquiring the name of hatred and Juana

Cannot bear the dread—the dark-jowl gaze of Sarge
Against her skin. Suddenly: bells go off again.
By the quiet effort of walking, three Mexican-

Types step in, whom Sarge refuses to serve...
Those gestures of his, those looks that could kill

A heart you carry in memory for years. A scene from
The past has caught me in the act of living: even
To myself I cannot say except with worried phrases
Upon a paper, how I withstood arrogance in a gruff
Voice coming with the deep-dyed colors of the screen;

How in the beginning I experienced almost nothing to
Say and now wonder if I can ever live enough to tell
The after-tale. I remember this and I remember myself
Locked into a back-row seat—I am a thin, flickering,
Helpless light, local-looking, unthought of at fourteen.

I

The 8 O'Clock Movie

Boston, 1973—Years had passed and I assumed a
Different life when one night, while resting from
Books on Marlborough Street (where things like
This can happen), there came into my room images

In black-and-white with a flow of light that
Would not die. It all came back to me in different
Terms: characters were born again, met up with
Each other in adult life, drifted across the

Screen to discover cattle and oil, traveled miles
On horseback in dust and heat, characters whose
Names emerged as if they mattered in a history
Book. Some were swept up by power and prejudice

Toward neighbors different from themselves,
Because that is what the picture is about, with
Class distinctions moving the plot along. A few
Could distinguish right from wrong; those who

Could not you condemned from the beginning when
You noticed them at all. Still others married or
Backed off from the ranch with poignant flair,
Like James Dean, who in the middle of grazing land

Unearthed the treasures of oil, buried his soul in
Money and went incoherent with alcohol. When the 40's
Came, two young men were drafted, the one called *Angel*
Dying at war. It's a generational tale, so everybody

Aged once more and said what they had to say along the
Way according to the script. And then the end: the
Hamburger joint brought into existence to the beat of
"The Yellow Rose of Texas," Juana and her child the

Color of dark amber, foreshadowing the Mexican-looking
Couple and their daughter, all in muteness, wanting
To be served. I climbed out of bed and in my head
Was a roaring of light—words spoken and unspoken

Had brought the obliterated back. Not again (I said,
From my second-floor room)...let this not be happening.
Three and-a-half hours had flicked by. As the sound
Trailed off into nothing, memory would not dissolve.

The Benedicts
(up-close)

Together with their daughter Luz, they
Are casually rich, self-assured, handsome—: have
Written their hoof-beats upon the land and

Named it; whose son is absent from this
Scene and is not a keeper of cows, but Harvard-trained
Instead, and thus a rebel who practices

The goodness of medicine alongside the
Ethnic good looks of his able nurse, Juana, who is
Here with her child trying to cross

The burning threshold of this pull-in café
And gets caught in the vast unwelcome which are the eyes
Of Sarge that fire upon the heart.

The Serving of Water

Tell the portly waitress to stay overtime and
She will do it. Dressed in white, she is a
Version of Sarge...Who follows orders well
...Who may have it in her mind she is "The

Sweetest little rosebud that Texas ever knew."
Her whole embodiment is whatever she is doing—:

At a booth, here, on the warm, sketchy plain
Of day, it is water she sets out for the
Benedicts: the measurement of water is a ritual
That isolates a face from the many colors of the

Day, and she does so with her eyes aimed at
Anyone she has given a harsh name to—like Juana,

And her child, half-Anglo, who in Juana's womb
Became all Mexican just the same. The waitress,
Entirely conscious of her act, whose eyes, quick,
Flee back to Sarge and now call out in silence,

Brings this moment to the edge of something tense
That spreads to everything. Her sudden look of

Outward regard—then Sarge, stirring dense cloud
Gathering *(entering left)*, standing over everyone
In tallness almighty. Ice-cream is what Rock Hudson
Wishes for his grandson: "Ice-cream it shall be,"

His words a revelation of delight: "Give the
Little fella some ice-cream"...Summer is one long

Afternoon when Sarge, moved by deep familiar
Wrath, talks down: "Ice-cream—thought that kid'd
Want a *tamale*." An angry mass of time travels
Back and forth the distance between Sarge and

Rock Hudson, as I sit, shy of speech, in a stammer
Of light, and breathe a breath not fully breathed...

Claiming the Air

Sarge, the proprietor, has already claimed the air with
His eyes, squared off against Rock Hudson by slurring
His grandchild. The camera's eye blinks, adjusts its

Focus to the segment that follows, the one grown around
Me like a lingering first cause. I remember it frame
By frame almost: *The little bell on top of the door is*

Heard, as the door opens: an old Mexican American couple,
And a woman, who could be an eldest daughter, come in.
Their image stays frozen, burns evenly around my brain: a
Tableau of himself, he is stooped in the ruts of old age,
Bits of gray hair fluffing out from under this hat, that

Courteous hat. The women, in uneventful-street clothes,
How their faces do not glow back from themselves, yet
Beckon with the color of sepia subdued—his also. Slow
In their gait toward the nearest booth by the door, they
Show a tired look as if from a journey begun long ago, one

Only their heritage could know. A woman I could be nephew
To and a couple old enough to call me grandson have walked
Into my life. They go unnoticed, except by Sarge, who walks

Among the greasy fires of his kitchen, comes to a stop and
Lets fly, heavy as lead: "Hey, you!" This is Sarge's Place,
A hamburger joint risen like a voice against the good.

Text for a
Vaquero: Flashback

Giant (1956), next-to-the-last scene: Old man Polo,
head *vaquero* on Rock Hudson's Reata Ranch, has come
from sunlight, wife and daughter with him, to break
bread, where hamburgers might be enough for a family
who shall not be served. In my other mind I see him
in his youthful air—:

Dawns were easy in the branding camps
when he scrambled up
to the restless movement of the herd.
And when morning had lifted into noon
he didn't choke on dust
because his lungs were stronger
than wind shifts.
He owned the language of a roundup
and each day experience triumphed on the range.

I see him riding with others:
sombreros *obeying the knowledge of the head;*
chaparreras *rough-riding*
with their legs.
He is straight-backed, bandana at the neck,
and a leather-brown face toughened by the sun
glancing off his sweat.
Now he's moving warily
around stampedes he still remembers
in his bones.
So that if, for an instant, he grows quieter,
it's because he remains a separate fact—
a silhouetted stoic in his saddle

like some vigilant bronzed-god
pondering his fate.

Evening draws upon the plain
and the cattle have been managed
into place. And it becomes almost like desire
when he reins his mount
before the mingled odors
of leather and foodstuff,
and beckons, in bated breath, a radiant sky
to show itself. Where the wind is cut off,
he lies with the flesh-tones of earth,
thinks about the history of the moon
and whether rain will come
to soothe the dust raving up from hooves
in the middle of July.
Bedded down, he's an object
half-buried among the blankets and the chaparral,
counting stars to fall asleep.
And when he dreams
he dreams that in a hundred years
his sons can own the ground he roams
and that his wife can be near...

That was many years ago. Now the trail has led
to here: the false hell of the hamburger place that
consumes him...where time denies him what he's been;
where there's no earth nor sky to make him free.

II

The Existence of Sarge

The old man places   his hat   on the table and
All three have sat down,   the same   as if their
Ancestors   had been   there first.   (Jump cut
To Sarge):   who is all at once by the booth in
Time   to hear the man   stricken   in years:
"Señor, buenos días." On this   earth where
Animals   have crawled into men, Sarge is tall
Among them,   well past six feet,   oppressive
Everywhere,   in a white shirt,   sleeves rolled
Up that declare   the beefiness   of his   arms
Which,   if extended, could reach across bodies
Of water.   He stands there   like God   of the
Plains country, heavy-footed   like a troglodyte,
And what he says   he says   with the weight of
A dozen churches   behind him: "You're in the
Wrong place, amigo. Come on,   let's get out of
Here. Vamoose. Ándale."   The old man, whose
Skin is second-stage bronze   from too much sun
That's gotten to it   and   won't pull back its
Color, has feebly   searched   among the
Threads of his pocket and extracted   the sum
Of his need. In quietude (etched in raw umber):
Reliquary   hands   are   endlessly   making   a
Wordless offering   in a coin purse.   Then the
Very way the tight-wound   voice   of Sarge
Echoes   through   the café walls, out onto the
Street,   and   back inside the Holiday Theater

Where I sit   alone   in the drop-shadows of the
Back—: "Your money is no good here.   Come on,
Let's go.   You too,"   he says to the women,
Their torment half inside me.   And with that:
He plops   the old man's hat on his head   and
Picks him   up by the lapels.   *Put the film*
In reverse (I think).   *Tear out these frames*
From time-motion and color;   run   the   words
Backward in Sarge's   breath   and sever   the
Tendons   of his thick   arms   in bold relief.

On the Subject of
Staying Whole

With orange soda and scoops of popcorn,
I have taken the vague wisdom of the
Body to my favorite last row seat at the
Movie house. It is 1956...and Sarge,
Keeper of the Lone Star house, Sarge,

Always Sarge, facing down everything
From the screen. I am fourteen and the
Muscles come to a stop: From the spell
Of too much make-believe world that is
Real. If I yell, "Nooooo!, noooo!,"

Would the projectionist stop the last
Reel of the machine? Would the audience
Rise up with me to rip down the screen?
I think now how it went: nothing was

Coming out of me that could choke off
The sentences of Sarge, a world-beater
Released into history I would later turn
Against. A second-skin had come over me

In a shimmer of color and light. I could
Not break free from the event that began
To inhabit me—gone was the way to dream

Outside myself. From inside, a small
Fire began to burn like deep doubt or

A world fallen...I held on. I held on.

Stop-Action:
Impression

Of course, the sanctity of the café,
The just-righteousness of the Place.
And Sarge, absolute, stressing the plane

Of outward fact, as when the screen
Gives up the deep-in-air-rooted sound
Of his voice, the strong ejectives

And glottals; as when he unifies his
Muscle with the blunt instrument of
His words with which he tries to purge

His roadside dominion, so that men and
Women by his side shall be cast out,
Left unregarded to their own. The eye

Gets insulted by light and the thought
Descends—: that Sarge, or someone
Like him, can banish you from this

Hamburger joint; from the rest of your
Life not yet entered; from this Holiday
Theater and all sense of place.

Fallingrief of
Unpleasure

The eye surrenders to the light and something begins
To go from you, as if you cannot but leave it: to

Wither on the floor, never to retrieve from darkness.
Like fragments of thought flashing, the slow burn of
Each frame rises into consciousness with the meaning

Of failed belief. A fallingrief of unpleasure grows
In you and something, call it the soul, deep is offended.
You want to go mad or die, but turn morose instead.

You lean back hard against your shadow and wish you
Could dissolve yourself in it, dissolve, fade to black.

Without a Prayer at
the Holiday Theater

What the screen had released through darkness was too
Much for a single afternoon. Without words, the child
Began to feel mortal, his mind breaking into awfulness:
A pulse-beat of dread worked itself down from his

Temples—there was, in his throat, a tightening dry
Knot and his mouth could not make spit. He longed
For something stronger than anything he was and the
Thought kept on him: why this was happening and where

He had failed. What had he been if not good all those
Years, off to Sunday school singing in the church
Choir? A wine-dark robe hung, brightly, in a
Practice room to prove it. Had the child been able

To ask nothing more of life than to turn desire into
Words he would have uttered—: *O Saviour, release*
me from this fear; give me cool waters to temper
the heat of this wound which the back-row darkness
hides. Send forth your swift light of compassion
into the places of my woe. Climb down and be seated
next to me, All-Merciful, bearer of the world's pain.
Increase the faith in me that your deep justice will
triumph on the screen. I need to see it done. Be
in me my rock and my redeemer, the Eternal Defender
of my soul. Mend now my spirit, O God, weaver of the
good, that I may walk away from here feeling whole.

III

Fight Scene
Beginning

Bick Benedict, that is, Rock Hudson in the
Time-clock of the movie, stands up and moves,
Deliberate, toward encounter. He has come out
Of the anxious blur of the backdrop, like

Coming out of the unreal into the world of
What's true, down to earth and distinct; has
Stepped up to Sarge, the younger of the two,

And would sure appreciate it if he: "Were a
Little more polite to these people." Sarge,
Who has something to defend, balks; asks
(*In a long-shot*) if: "that there papoose down

There, his name Benedict too?," by which he
Means one-year old Jordy in the background
Booth hidden in the bosom of mother love of

Juana, who listens, trying not to listen. Rock
Hudson, his hair already the color of slate,
Who could not foresee this challenge, arms
Akimbo (*turning around*), contemplates the stable

And straight line of years gone by, says: "Yeah,
Come to think of it, it *is*." And so acknowledges,
In his heart, his grandson, half-Anglo, half-

Brown. Sarge repents from words, but no
Part of his real self succumbs: "All right—
Forget I asked you. Now you just go back
Over there and sit down and we ain't gonna

Have no trouble. But this bunch here is
Gonna eat somewhere's else." Never shall I
Forget, never how quickly his hand threw my

Breathing off—how quickly he plopped the
Hat heavily askew once more on the old
Man's head, seized two fistsful of shirt and
Coat and lifted his slight body like nothing,

A no-thing, who could have been any of us,
Weightless nobodies bronzed by real-time far
Off somewhere, not here, but in another

Country, yet here, where Rock Hudson's face
Deepens; where in one motion, swift as a
Miracle, he catches Sarge off guard, grabs
His arm somehow, tumbles him back against

The counter and draws fire from Sarge to
Begin the fight up and down the wide screen
Of memory, ablaze in Warner-color light.

Fight Scene,
Part II

Mad-eyed Sarge recovers with a vengeance, tears
Away his white apron, lays bare his words: "You're
Outta line, mister..." And there are no more words

To say when he crouches forward at the same time
That one punch crashes him rearward among the table
And chairs by the jukebox that breaks out into the

Drumming of "The Yellow Rose of Texas," who was,
It is said, dark-eyed herself. In the dynasty of
Towering men—: all height, all live weight has
Evolved into Sarge, who stays etched in my eye as when

He parts the air with a right cross...and Rock Hudson
Begins to fall, is falling, falls in the slackening
Way of a slow weep of a body collapsing, hitting

The floor like falling to the rocky earth, territory
To justice being what Sarge refuses to give up.
Rock Hudson, in the name of Bick Benedict, draws
Himself up, though clearly, the holding muscles of
His legs are giving out—one moment he is in a

Clinch with Sarge, the next he is rammed back
Against the red booths. The two of them have
Mobilized their arms that breed fire, and so it

Goes: a right upper-cut to Sarge and a jab to
Rock Hudson, engaged in a struggle fought in the
Air and time of long ago and was fought again this

Morning at dawn when light fell upon darkness and
Things were made right again. (I shut, now, slowly,

My eyes, and see myself seeing, as in a frame within
A frame, two fighters set upon each other. To this
Day I contend that I saw, for a second, the whole

Screen fill up with the arm-fist of Sarge blurring
Across it.) Now the fighters are one with the loud
Music bruising the eardrums. To be injured, there
Must be blood to see, for they have become two minds

Settling a border dispute. Two men have organized
Their violence to include me, as I am on the side
Of Rock Hudson, but carry nothing to the fight but

Expectations that, when it is over, I can repeat the
Name of goodness in Sarge's Place, as the singers sing
That raging song that seems to keep the fight alive.

Fight Scene:
Final Frames

...And now it must end. Sarge with too much muscle,
Too much brawn against Bick Benedict with his half-idea
To stay alive in the fight, but his shoulders, all down
To his arms, can no longer contend to come back, cannot
Intercept the wallop that up-vaults him over the counter,

As over a line in a house divided at heart. He steadies
Himself upward, all sense of being there gone, to meet
Sarge (*upwards shooting-angle*), standing with fists
Cocked to strike and he does, once more and again. You
Can see and can hear Rock Hudson's daughter give out a

Long-suffering cry, "Daaaddyyy!," and for Sarge to "leave
Him alooonnne!" But in a wrath like this there can be no
Pity upon the earth, as the blows come harder from Sarge
Like a fever in him. Then it happens: Sarge's one last,
Vital, round-arm punch, one just measure of power, turning

The concept of struggle around. The earth, finally, is
Cleared of goodness when Rock Hudson is driven to the
Rugged floor and does not rise, his wife, Elizabeth
Taylor (Leslie), kneeling to be with his half-life,
Illuminated body and heartbeat. Whose heartbeat? Whose

Strength must be summoned to make his graceful body
Arise? Who shall come forth and be followed? What
Name do I give thoughts that collapse through each
Other? When may I learn strongly to act, who am caught
In this light like a still photograph? Can two fighters

Bring out a third? To live, must I learn how to die?
Sarge stands alone now, with all the atoms of his power
Still wanting to beat the air, stands in glory like a
Law that stands for other laws. It remains with me:
That a victory is not over until you turn it into words;

That a victor of his kind must legitimize his fists
Always, so he rips from the wall a sign, like a writ
Revealed tossed down to the strained chest of Rock Hudson.
And what he said unto him, he said like a pulpit preacher
Who knows only the unfriendly parts of the Bible,

After all, Sarge is not a Christian name. The camera
Zooms in:
                    WE RESERVE
                    THE RIGHT
                TO REFUSE SERVICE
                    TO ANYONE

In the dream-work of the scene, as it is in memory, or
In a pattern with a beginning and an end only to begin
Again, timing is everything. Dissolve and the music ends.

IV

The Trailing Consequence: A Triptych

I

Journey Home

The picture show, three-and-a-half hours of it,
was over;
the credits, so many,
ascended into immortality.

The fiery art of film
had sent my head buzzing—:
I arose in penumbra, vexed at the unwinding
course of truth and was now lost in my steps,
eyes struggling with unnatural chasms of light.
I walked home for a long time
and in my mind   I regarded
the tall screen bearing down on me—
I was drifting away
from its outburst, yet its measure of violence,
like an indictment from Sarge,
did not fade.

There was no wind.
No firm star came out
to acquire me in safety.
The world seemed enormous around me
and as I moved in it
I felt I could not journey
further than myself.

Minutes passed
and then another.
(Once I saw, as in a dream,
that I had never reached home.)
I crossed the railroad tracks, went past
the lumber yard, the concrete bridge at Purgatory Creek,
and over a second set of tracks—
a weary logic leading me back to where I began.
I think I must have made a fist
in desperation, as tough as the years
to my name
and there grew in my mouth
a great shout which never came.

Time and time over: a child at that age
falls short of endowing dumb misery with speech.

II
Observer and Observed

No one walks with me
(down the dust-bound street
where I step lightly),
sullen, slight-young boy.
Each neighbor,
in the ease of the afternoon
serenely grown out of something forgetful,
looks through me,
believing life goes on as before
as I pass by.
The trees and the houses among them
see me staring in muteness;
from where they stand—houses, trees,
neighbors—they cannot know
the sudden intake of all breath,
a sigh I myself do not comprehend.

Something weightless
gathers around me, while my body, unpoised,
holds its forward momentum
in silence and slow time.

As the afternoon   emptied of meaning

deepens perceptibly,

the soft-hollowed steps in which I move
are my only cause.

III
Dusk with Dreaming

The neighborhood, 1956—:
I reached its border
feeling I was nothing
other than my name.
It seems a long time ago
that I stepped into the *patio*,
held off for a moment
before going in for supper
and leaned, instead,
against a pecan tree's
slender-rooted trunk.
And standing at my point of view,
I felt a nothingness
burning through all thought.

By now the day was fading into twilight,
and I beginning
not to cast a shadow where I had always been,
when I saw,
suddenly, a boy alone
who had to tear to prove he was...
Something from the movie screen had
dropped into life, his small shield of faith
no longer with him.

Dusk was dawning over the tree-tops
when I was called inside
where grace was said, I am sure of it,
for we were always grateful to the sky.
I remember the clock ticking

and my breathing

when finally

my mouth took ethnically again
sustenance in solace.
The rest of me began to dream and my mind
flew off and I became, for that instant:

another boy from another land, in another time,
another time, which is also home.

V

That Autumn

The movie came to a close and went, and, in time,
it was forgotten, placed upon the background of
the past—: and I returned to play and laughter,

to class and lessons hardly learned. Each time I
spoke I lost a thought, or else said nothing to
friends who might have seen the picture to the end;
who might have been awakened, transfigured in some

faint and inner way by rage. Now I think: *the
poem's the thing wherein I'll etch the semblance
of the film.* So the mind becomes involved again with
after-sight, with frames as large as screens...and

without wearing it as too much knowledge, something
out of reach gets under way and the two-sided act of
myself (in the available light) behaves into words...

Fade-Out-Fade-In

From the screen, from its multi-colored light
that struck my face and eye's anatomy, I
understood the indigenous fact—a victory for
Sarge, who disrupted my poise; who reached me,
heavily, through the shadows banked against the
back-most seats. When goodness was torn down
amidst the café air, not breathable at times,
something happened in me as well. With the vivid
plain before me at film's end, before the curtains

closed, the bright blankness of the screen came
down and shone on me when I stepped into the
aisle, vague in the yielding chiaroscuro. And
what I took in that afternoon took root and a
quiet vehemence arose. It arose in language—
the legitimate deduction of the years thought out.
Now I am because I write: I know it in my heart
and know it in the sound iambics of my fist that
mark across the paper with the sun's exacting rays.

The Slow Weight
of Time

Endlessly to no end looking through
memory (O conscience that accentuates
a history full of ways to know the

heart) at what not long ago did happen,
you turn back to when your offended
little world was unresolved. Each

thought is longing to become another,
longing to sing, once again and always,
deep into a song of what memory still

might know. You draw air, press these
thoughts to paper and release your daily
self from the lost fragments of the past.

Now: in the conquered vigil of your
days, all distance weeps for you as you
drift out from the journey through

the slow weight of time, and you claim
that you are safe forever in the
very words you have chosen to become.

The Telling

Anywhere, anytime, I fix it in my mind
    that what I know and runs through the
body, like unction, is anxious truth in me:

truth, uproaring in shadow and light,
which descends from days burnt away nakedly;

from what the eye has taken in, and the eye
    does not confuse time and place with
the act. At this moment of being human

(when the teller is the tale being told),
the ash of memory rises that I might speak,

that I might tell what I tell with words,
    which are the past falling from my mind.
Let the script reveal: that in the telling

I am cast in time forward, wherethrough runs
the present—one track of light triumphant,

the sum of everything that ignites this room
    with life, *vida que no olvida,* calling out
my name...O life, this body that speaks, this

repetitious self drawn out from *la vida revivida,*
vida sacada de cada clamor. Home at last, I am

trusting the light that attends me, and the
    natural physic of breathing, with words to
show the measure. *O vida vivida y por venir...*

notes

"The Serving of Water": *tamale,* from *tamal,* a Mexican and Mexican American dish made of corn dough, a filling (usually meat) and seasonings, wrapped in presoaked corn husks and steamed.

"Text for a *Vaquero:* Flashback": *vaquero,* cowboy; *sombreros,* hats; *chaparreras,* chaps, i.e., leather leg overalls, without a seat, worn by cowboys over normal trousers; *chaparral,* a dense growth of shrubs and trees (southwestern United States and Mexico).

"The Existence of Sarge": *"Señor, buenos días." "Sir, good morning." "Amigo,"* friend; *Vamoose. Ándale.* Get out of here. Hurry (Go).

"The Telling": last three stanzas:

the sum of everything that ignites this room
    with life, *life that forgets not,* calling out
my name...O life, this body that speaks, this

repetitious self drawn out from *life relived,*
life rescued from each uproar. Home at last, I am

trusting the light that attends me, and the
    natural physic of breathing, with words to
show the measure. *O life lived and life left to live...*

Tino Villanueva

Born on December 11, 1941 in San Marcos, Texas, Tino Villanueva has had a diversity of work experiences before his formal college education, ranging from migrant worker to assembly-line construction of furniture in his native hometown. After two years as an Army supply clerk in the Panama Canal Zone, he returned and attended, under the G. I. Bill, Southwest Texas State University in San Marcos where he received his B. A. in Spanish and English in 1969. He was a graduate fellow at SUNY-Buffalo for which he received an M. A. in 1971, moving then to Boston University where in 1981 he completed his doctoral dissertation on contemporary Spanish poetry in the Department of Modern Foreign Languages & Literatures. In 1978-1979 he was a recipient of the Ford Foundation Graduate Fellowship. In addition to currently serving as Preceptor in Spanish at Boston University, Villanueva is the founder of Imagine Publishers, Inc., and editor of *Imagine: International Chicano Poetry Journal*. He is the author of three collections of poetry, *Hay Otra Voz Poems (1972)*, *Shaking Off the Dark* (1984) and *Crónica de mis años peores* (1987). Villanueva has been painting since 1973. His art work has been exhibited in El Paso, West Berlin, Boston, and most recently on the covers of *Green Mountains Review* and *TriQuarterly*.